Mandalas Coloring Books for Adults
A Coloring Book for Adults

Jason S. Blankenship

Mandalas Coloring Books for Adults
A Coloring Book for Adults

Copyright: Published in the United States by Jason S. Blankenship
Published July 2016

All rights reserved. No part of this publication may be reproduced, stored in retrieval system, copied in any form or by any means, electronic, mechanical, photocopying, recording or otherwise transmitted without written permission from the publisher. Please do not participate in or encourage piracy of this material in any way. You must not circulate this book in any format. Jason S. Blankenship does not control or direct users' actions and is not responsible for the information or content shared, harm and/or actions of the book readers.

ISBN-13: 978-1535463041

ISBN-10: 153546304X

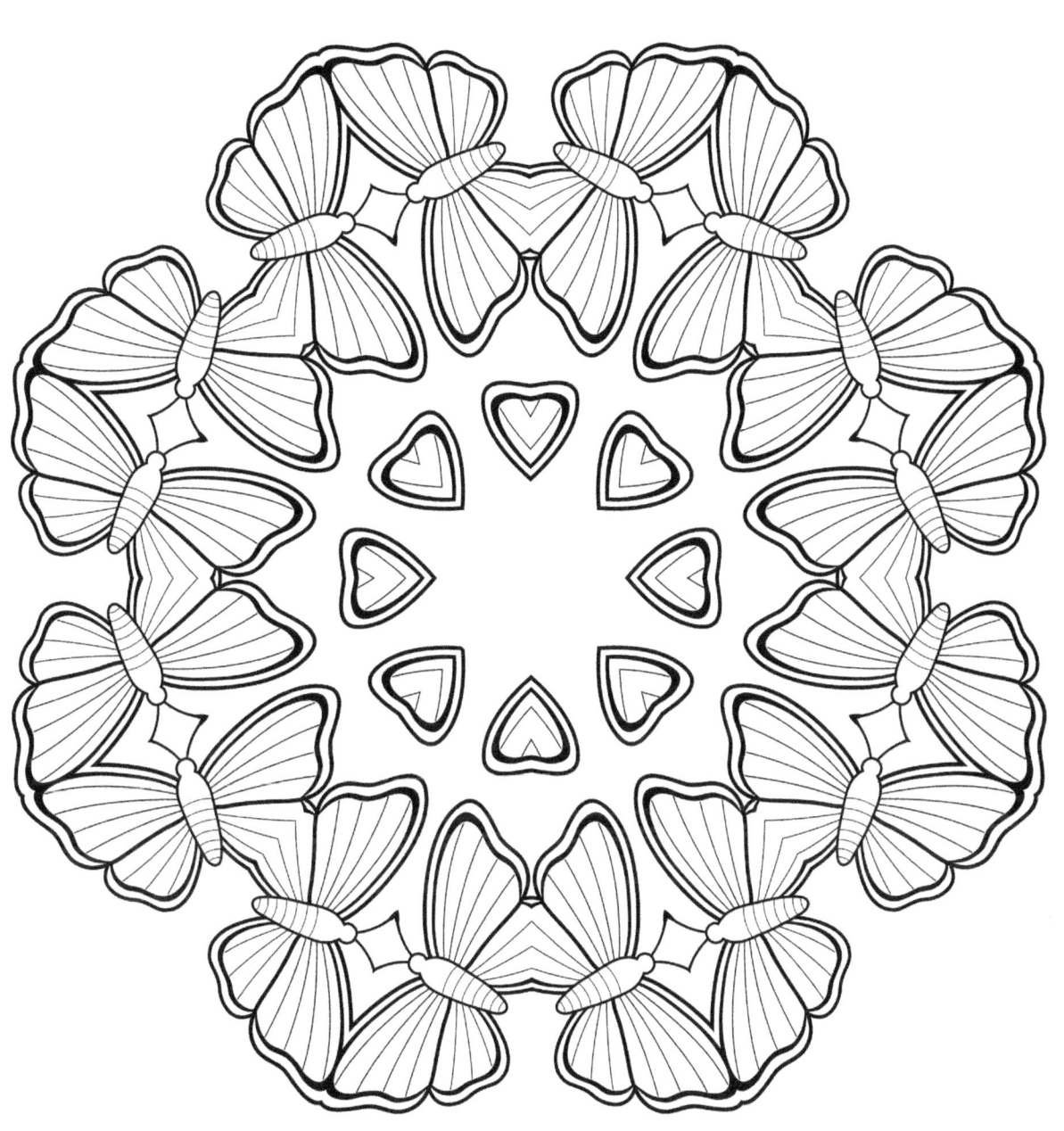

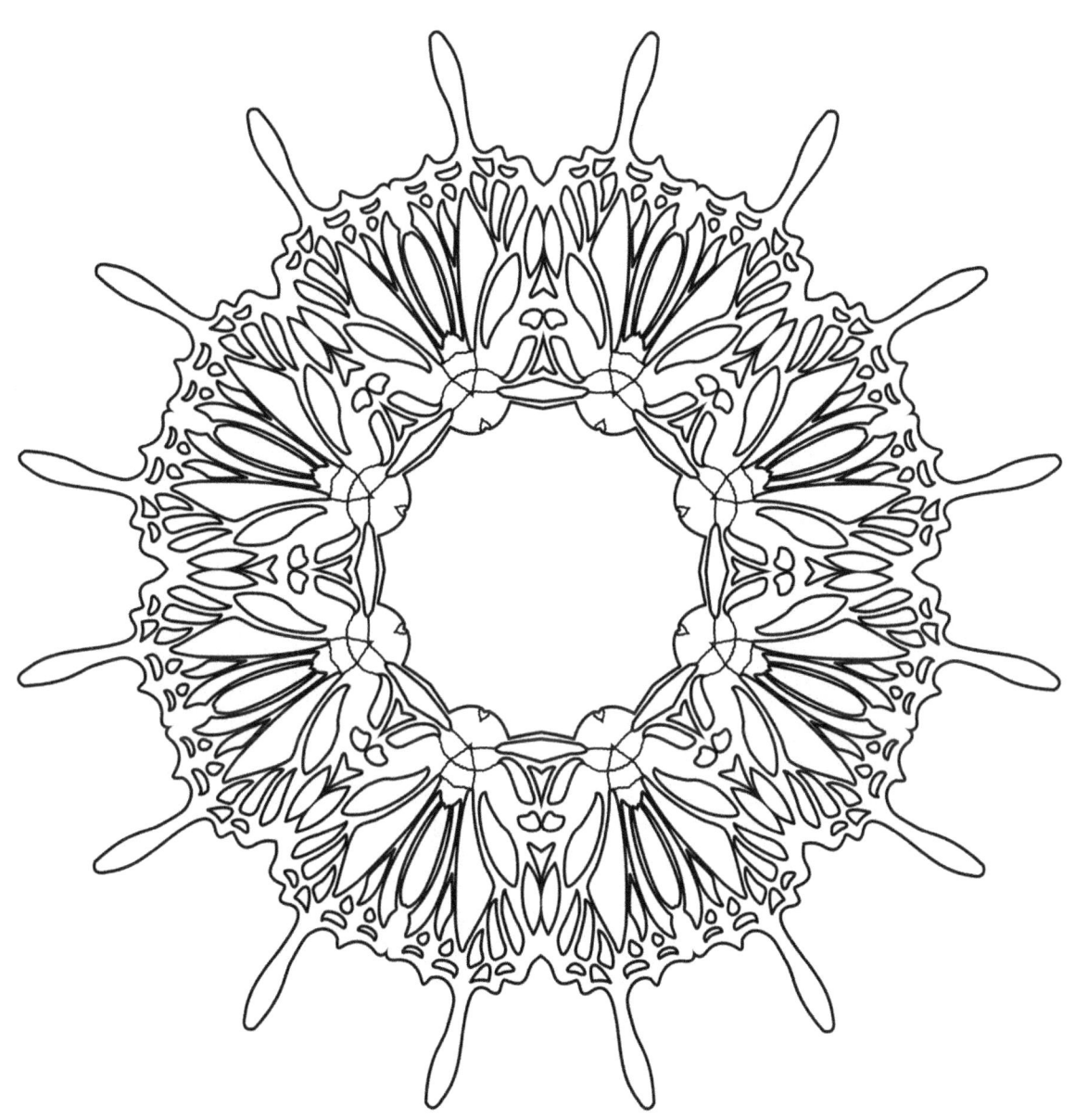

www.ingramcontent.com/pod-product-compliance
Lightning Source LLC
Chambersburg PA
CBHW080709190526
45169CB00006B/2309